BACKSTREET BOYS
CAUGHT ON CAMERA
BY TOP OF THE POPs

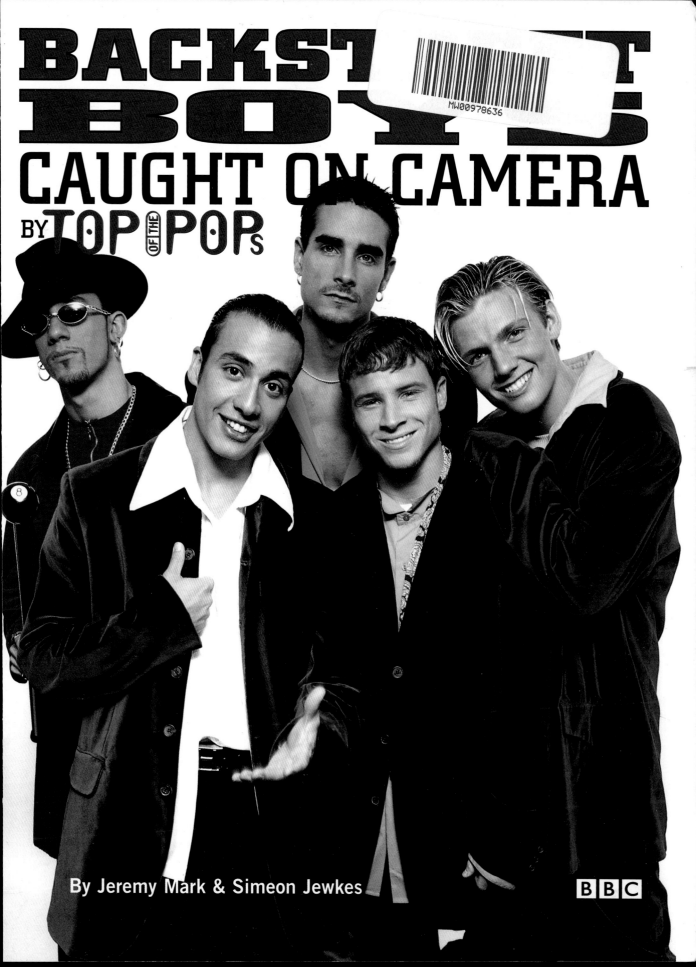

By Jeremy Mark & Simeon Jewkes

BBC

Top Of The Pops Backstreet Boys Caught On Camera
First published in 1998 by BBC Worldwide Ltd
Woodlands, 80 Wood Lane, London W12 OTT

Based on material from *Top Of The Pops Magazine* and
Live & Kicking Magazine.

ISBN 0 563 38090 X

Colour Origination by Kestrel Digital Colour.

Printed by Jarrold Book Printing.

AJ
NICK
BRIAN
KEVIN
HOWIE
BACKSTREET BOYS
CAUGHT ON CAMERA

AJ

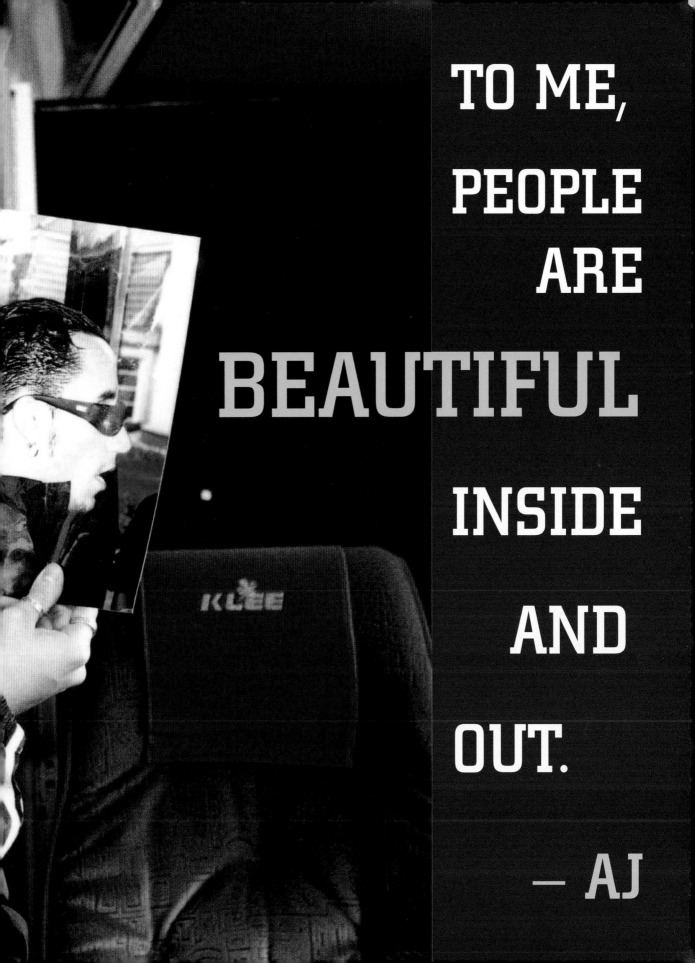

TO ME, PEOPLE ARE **BEAUTIFUL** INSIDE AND OUT.

— AJ

AJ gets picked on a lot by the rest of us, but he brings it on himself. We have specific rules and stuff which he sometimes doesn't like to follow. He's a bit of a rebel, our AJ.

— KEVIN

I like to make people happy and please everyone at the same time, but it's not easy. I've got a really big heart, but sometimes it gets in the way and I trip over it. — AJ

THE WILDEST BACKSTREET BOY? WELL, THAT'S GOTTA BE ME. I'M ALWAYS CHANGING

THE WAY I LOOK, LIKE DYING MY HAIR, GROWING A GOATEE. BUT I LIKE TO THINK IT'S

MORE ABOUT BEING CREATIVE AND SPONTANEOUS THAN BEING A REBEL. — AJ

Nick

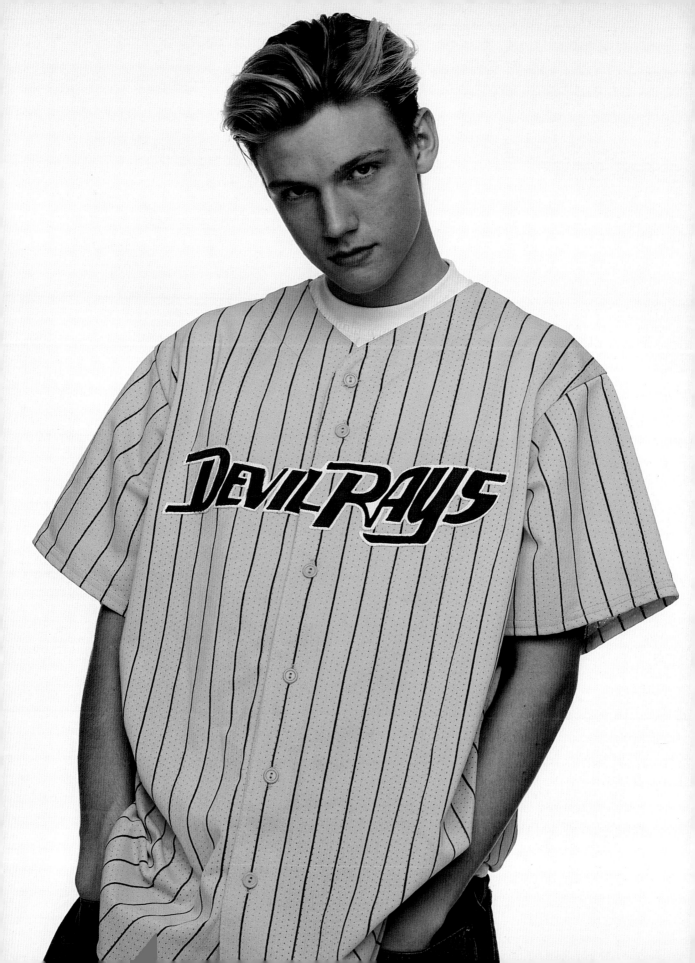

I HAVE A VERY ARTISTIC NATURE. I LOVE TO DRAW. I'VE A WICKED IMAGINATION! — NICK

I GUESS I HAVE MISSED OUT ON CERTAIN THINGS BECAUSE I JOINED THE BAND SO YOUNG THE GUYS ARE ALWAYS TELLING ME ABOUT ALL THE THINGS THEY DID AT HIGH SCHOOL – LIKE PLAYING FOOTBALL, GOING TO THE PROM, GRADUATING AND STUFF. BUT YOU KNOW, I'M PLEASED I'VE MADE THIS CHOICE AND THE SACRIFICES AREN'T SO BAD.
— NICK

I last cried when we visited a children's hospital. It made me really, really sad. But I didn't let anyone know I'd cried as I don't like to show my innermost feelings.
— Nick

I FIND IT REALLY EMBARRASSING TALKING ABOUT GIRLS AND STUFF LIKE THAT. — NICK

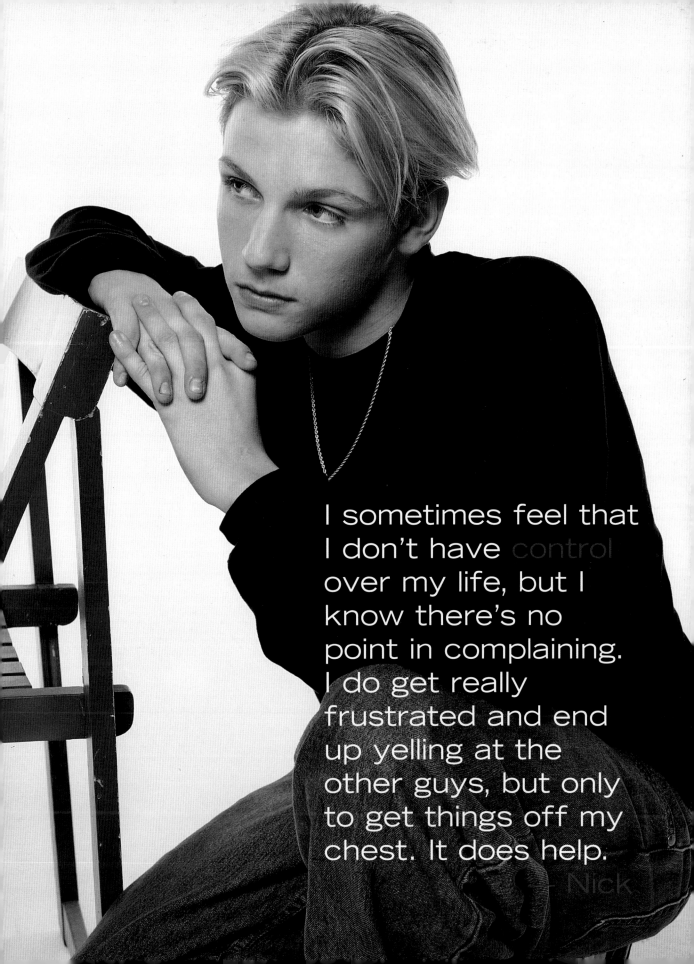

I sometimes feel that I don't have control over my life, but I know there's no point in complaining. I do get really frustrated and end up yelling at the other guys, but only to get things off my chest. It does help.

Nick

The girls at school thought I was a bit odd.

I got asked out a bunch of times though, which was cool. I like girls asking me out because it takes the pressure off my having to do it.   — Nick

IT'S KINDA WEIRD HAVING GIRLS SWOONING OVER ME, BUT I'D BE LYING IF I SAID I DIDN'T ENJOY IT. I REMEMBER WHEN I WAS IN SCHOOL IT WAS A REAL TASK TRYING TO GET A GIRLFRIEND, BUT NOW THERE ARE GIRLS ASKING ME OUT ALL OVER. IT'S A TOTAL TURNAROUND.

— NICK

I don't have a special kissing technique or anything. I just do whatever comes naturally. It's been a long time since I've kissed anyone though, so I'm way out of practice at the moment.

— Nick

Brian

Have I ever snogged a fan? Well, not intentionally. One time though, I was singing I'll Never Break Your Heart on stage and went down to the audience and sang to this girl who'd been staring at me the whole time. When I'd finished the song, I went to give her a kiss on the cheek, but she tried to slip her tongue down my throat — right in front of everybody! I was completely dumbstruck!

— Brian

I THINK I'D MAKE A LOVING, **CARING**, UNDERSTANDING BOYFRIEND, WHO'S IN TOUCH WITH HIS EMOTIONS. OR AT LEAST I'D LIKE TO BE. — **BRIAN**

NICK'S LIKE THE BABY BROTHER I NEVER HAD. I LOOK OUT FOR HIM AND HELP HIM IN ANY WAY I CAN. — BRIAN

ME AND BRIAN ARE REAL GOOD FRIENDS — AS CLOSE AS BROTHERS. WE EVEN TALK ABOUT BUYING HOUSES NEXT DOOR TO EACH OTHER. — NICK

I WAS DATING THIS GIRL AND I WENT TO HER SCHOOL AND PUT A DOZEN ROSES IN HER LOCKER, SO THEY WERE THE FIRST THING SHE SAW THAT MORNING. THEY DIDN'T EXACTLY FALL ON TOP OF HER, BUT SHE WAS VERY SURPRISED.   – BRIAN

I'm really happy. All that's happened to me isn't quite what I expected at all. We're not just another boy band. We're here to stay and we want the world.
— Brian

I've always tried to
be funny, or
stupid, or whatever.
I love making
people laugh and I
think it comes quite
naturally to me.
— Brian

I THINK YOU HAVE TO TAKE LIFE DAY BY DAY, AND THE MORE HUMOUR YOU FIND IN EVERYDAY THINGS, THEN THE HAPPIER YOU'LL BE. — BRIAN

THE GOOD OLD DAYS! :O)

Kevin

I've learned from our travels that no matter where you are, people are pretty much the same. Everyone just wants to be happy and if more people realised that, then the world would be a far nicer place.
— Kevin

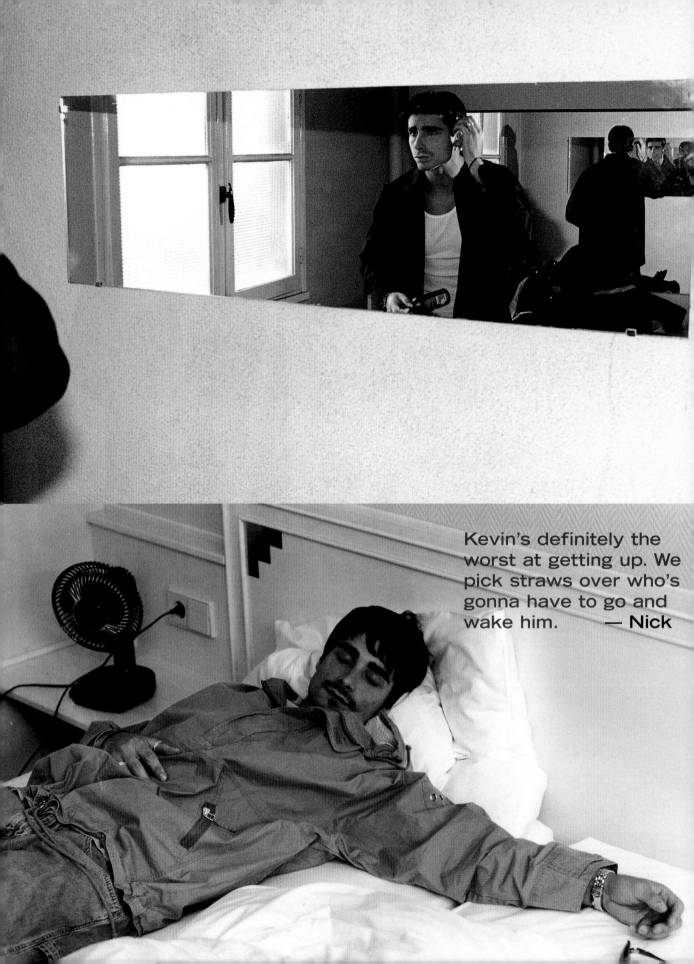

Kevin's definitely the worst at getting up. We pick straws over who's gonna have to go and wake him. — Nick

KEVIN IS REALLY MATURE, RESPONSIBLE AND **AMBITIOUS**. HE KNOWS WHAT HE WANTS. HE'S A BORN LEADER AND KEEPS US ALL TOGETHER.

— **HOWIE**

Being a perfectionist is probably my best quality and my worst. I just really want Backstreet Boys to be the best we can and in rehearsals I'll make us practice again and again until it's good enough.
— Kevin

I'm kinda the big brother, being the oldest, so I try to keep everyone in line. I can be a little rough on the chaps, but they know I don't mean it.
— Kevin

Howie

I PREFER TO TALK FROM THE HEART AND GO WITH THE WAY I FEEL. A FEW PEOPLE
HAVE TOLD ME THEY FIND IT WARMING AND ROMANTIC.   — HOWIE

NOT BEING LOVED FRIGHTENS ME. I'M A VERY LOVING PERSON AND FOR ME TO GIVE OUT SO MUCH LOVE — AND NOT RECEIVE ANY IN RETURN — REALLY SCARES ME. — HOWIE

I've had my heart broken a couple of times, unfortunately. It was when my last two relationships ended. Neither of them could deal with my career. I respect them for being honest, but it still hurt.

— Howie

HOWIE'S KIND OF A PERFECTIONIST WHEN IT COMES TO HIS LOOKS. HE HAS TO MAKE SURE HE'S SPOTLESS BEFORE HE LEAVES HIS ROOM AND SPENDS A BIT TOO MUCH TIME ON HIS APPEARANCE. WE'RE LIKE, 'IT'S OK HOWIE, YOUR 34TH HAIR IS IN PLACE!'

I'VE LEARNED A LOT

OVER THE PAST FEW

YEARS. I SAY WHAT'S

ON MY MIND A LOT

MORE NOW AND

I'M NOT SCARED

OF WHAT PEOPLE

THINK OF ME.

— HOWIE

I can't even begin to think about **Backstreet Boys** ever ending. We're already having **so much fun** and we've really only just started out.
— **Howie**

DON'T MISS

TOP OF THE POPS MAGAZINE
EVERY MONTH

AVAILABLE

FROM ALL GOOD

NEWSAGENTS